Mary's Beads

of

Transformation

by Patricia M. McCormack, Ed.D.

Liguori

ONE LIGUORI DRIVE
LIGUORI MO 63057-9999

Imprimi Potest:
Richard Thibodeau, C.Ss.R.
Provincial, Denver Province
The Redemptorists

ISBN 0-7648-1020-0
Library of Congress Catalog Number: 2002117249

© 2003, Liguori Publications
Printed in the United States of America
03 04 05 06 07 5 4 3 2 1

All Scripture quotations are from the *Christian Community Bible*, Catholic Pastoral Edition, © 1995, Liguori Publications. All rights reserved.

To order, call 1-800-325-9521
www.liguori.org
www.catholicbooksonline.com

Contents

Introduction:
What Kind of Rosary Is This?

Today most organizations create mission statements to set the direction or goal of their activities and to suggest the most advantageous way of achieving that goal. If we read the concluding prayer of the rosary as if it were a mission statement, what does it suggest about the goal of praying the rosary? And what does it say is the means of achieving that goal?

O God, whose only begotten Son by his life, death, and resurrection has purchased for us the rewards of eternal life, grant, we beseech you, that while meditating upon these mysteries [means] of the holy rosary of the Blessed Virgin Mary, we may imitate what they contain and obtain what they promise [goal], through the same Christ, Our Lord. Amen

The Transforming Power of Prayer

When we imitate the virtue, attitudes, and spiritual qualities of the Jesus we find in the gospels, we are transformed. Praying the rosary (and other forms of prayer) can transform us ever more clearly into the image God created. Praying is the means, transformation is the goal. We were created as expressions of God, gifted with the ability to choose (intellect) and the ability to love (free will). But our limitations cover the God-image in us with layers of separation. Transformation is the process of cooperating with God to remove the separation, allowing Christ to be revealed in us and conforming us to his will for us. Prayer is divine conversation that shapes the human heart to recognize the attitudes and desires of Jesus, to respond to them, and to allow them to become our pattern for human living.

Prayer transforms. In the process of transformation, nothing of the stuff of our lives is wasted. God uses all to uncover in us the gift that God created. Even our sinfulness, mistakes, and woundedness, given over to Christ, become redeemed parts of our true selves and teach us to resonate with the words, "When I am weak, then I am strong" (2 Corinthians 12:10b).

Once I watched a young friend at play, twisting pieces of a dinosaur replica. I concluded that he was breaking the toy. When my friend saw my distress, he countered it by saying, "Don't worry. Look! You are supposed to do this." Sure enough, he had reconfigured the dinosaur into a spaceship. No pieces were eliminated. They were merely reconfigured into a spaceship. Similarly, by the grace of God, parts of our selves that we reject, resist, dislike, and try to disown can become building blocks of our redemption. Prayer helps us to recognize those parts and to reconcile them to the will of God, thus yielding to God's transformative plan.

As we use the structure of the rosary to meditate on the life of Christ, we receive guidance for our souls. Through, with, and in Mary, we explore the challenges and life-giving responses of Jesus, Mary, and many others—Joseph, Elizabeth, the angels, the shepherds, the Magi, Simeon, Anna, the apostles, Simon the Cyrenian, the faithful women, a thief on a cross, Nicodemus, Joseph of Arimathea, and Mary Magdalene, to name a few. While meditating upon these mysteries, we receive direction for discipleship.

The mysteries of the rosary also provide a context in which to name, claim, and tame some of the life-blocking aspects of our own selves that we find in figures like Herod, Pilate, corrupt or mediocre spiritual leaders, bullying soldiers, Peter in his weakness, traitor Judas, doubting Thomas, ambitious apostles, or jeering, ungrateful citizens who shout "Crucify him!" (Mark 15:13). At these times, the rosary gives us a chance to identify with the humanity of gospel figures. We can also be challenged, comforted, or stretched by the words of Jesus and the dynamics contained in the mysteries, for example, how to deal with interruptions to our plans (annunciations), initiate response to the needs of others (visitations), recognize and respond to epiphany experiences (presentations), embrace the cross in our life journey (crucifixions), or accept death to self and bury past hurts so as to rise transformed in Christ (resurrections). All aspects of the mysteries of the rosary are contained within our souls and useful to our growth in holiness. With Mary as mother, mentor, and model, our meditation on the mysteries leads to our transformation into the image of her son.

How to Pray this Rosary

To achieve this goal, I suggest a creative style of rosary prayer. After Vatican II, Rome commissioned a study, summarized in "The Rosary, Gospel of Joy," *(Cross and Crown,* 1969) by Père Eyquem, O.P., of the National Center of the Rosary in France. He proposes a simple approach to the rosary that respects tradition, theology, and psychology. This way of praying the rosary emphasizes Jesus as the focus of each bead. Each Hail Mary begins with the words of the Angel Gabriel and Elizabeth. Then a scriptural reference completes each bead. The prayer of petition, "Holy Mary, Mother of God ...," which originated in the fifteenth-century Church, is reserved for the end of each decade. Father

Eyquem suggests substituting the word *Rejoice* for *Hail*, because it "helps us to place ourselves in a Messianic perspective, which was Mary's personal attitude" (p. 290). Here are some examples:

* Rejoice Mary, full of grace, the Lord is with you. Blessed are you among women and blessed is the fruit of your womb, Jesus, who was scourged, mocked, and spit upon.
* Rejoice Mary, full of grace, the Lord is with you. Blessed are you among women and blessed is the fruit of your womb, Jesus, who said, "I am the way, the truth and the life" (John 14:6a).
* Rejoice Mary, full of grace, the Lord is with you. Blessed are you among women and blessed is the fruit of your womb, Jesus, of whom it was said, "He has done all things well; he makes the deaf hear and the dumb speak" (Mark 7:37).

The scholars of the French National Center of the Rosary remind their readers that Mary's intention is always to reveal her son. This style of meditation on the mysteries promotes Mary's intention because it leads us to Jesus through Mary. Possibilities are endless with this Marian devotion. This pamphlet merely introduces the reader to the prayer style, illustrates the breadth of variation, and urges the reader to cooperate with the promptings of the Holy Spirit to build on this model during times of private prayer. Here are some possibilities:

- Each bead could vary within a decade or mystery.
- Each mystery of ten beads could be an experience in meditation.
- New mysteries could expand the traditional fifteen and the pope's Mysteries of Light, for example, the Sermon on the Mount or the encounter with Zacchaeus.
- An entire rosary of one mystery, the life of Jesus, could evolve.
- Each bead could recall words that Jesus spoke to us, for example, "…Jesus, who said, 'Come, follow me.'"

- With Scripture as reference, each bead could contain action statements, for example, "…Jesus, who cured the paralytic; who raised Lazarus from the dead; who invited himself to the house of Zacchaeus," and many others.
- Walk the Way of the Cross with rosary in hand and use the stations to prompt you, for example, "…Jesus, who was stripped of his garments; who fell a second time under the weight of the cross," and so on.

Meditating on the mysteries of the lives of Jesus and Mary and applying those messages to daily living is the ageless purpose of the rosary. Prayed with intentionality, the rosary is a means of transformation into the image of Christ. The concluding prayer of the traditional rosary says it well: "while *meditating* upon these mysteries of the most holy rosary of the Blessed Virgin Mary, we may *imitate* what they contain and *obtain* what they promise." May this be so!

Summary of the Prayer

1. Begin in the usual way, with the Sign of the Cross and the Apostles' Creed, the Lord's Prayer, and three traditional Hail Marys followed by the Glory Be.

2. If you wish to pray the pope's new Mysteries of Light, for example, turn to page 23, and spend a brief quiet time considering the Transformational Moments for the first mystery, Jesus' Baptism. (The suggestions in the Transformational Moments allow you to connect your life today with the lives of Jesus and Mary.) What in your life resonates with these suggestions? If none of the suggestions connect with your current circumstances, in what way does your life connect with the mystery?

3. Hold this connection in your heart as you begin to pray the beads. Announce the first mystery, pray the Lord's Prayer, and then begin the decade. Each bead begins "Rejoice Mary, full of grace, the Lord is with you. Blessed are you among women

and blessed is the fruit of your womb, Jesus," and concludes with the text for each bead, for example, the first bead for this mystery is "about whom the Baptist said, 'I baptize you in water as a sign of your conversion, but the one who is coming after me is more powerful than me; indeed I am not worthy to carry his sandals. He will baptize you in the Holy Spirit and fire'" (Matthew 3:11). You may pause after each bead to allow the scriptural reference to sink into your heart and soul.

4. Conclude the decade by praying "Holy Mary, Mother of God, pray for us sinners, now, and at the hour of our death" at the end of the tenth bead. Follow with a Glory Be, an announcement of the next mystery, a short meditation on the transformational moments, and the Lord's Prayer. Then begin the process of praying the next decade. Repeat until the rosary is completed, and conclude in your customary way.

You will begin praying this rosary smoothly at some point during your first attempt. Please remember that there is no wrong way to pray the rosary.

The Joyful Mysteries

First Joyful Mystery: Annunciation

Transformational Moments

Unexpected interruptions to your plans; unlikely messengers; detours that take you into a limbo existence or into 180-degree turns; trusting dream messages; feeling the weight of life decisions; knowing a power beyond yourself; accepting the invitation and challenge to be a Christ-bearer; facing the unknown; being the messenger of transformative news to another; replacing fear with trust; embracing the mission of safeguarding the Christ within another; seeking spiritual direction to discern the voice within

Rejoice Mary, full of grace, the Lord is with you. Blessed are you among women and blessed is the fruit of your womb, Jesus,

* who was sent at the time God appointed
* whose messenger was sent to Nazareth, a town of Galilee
* whose angel addressed you, a virgin betrothed to Joseph of the house of David
* whose messenger greeted you as the favored one (see Luke 1:28)
* whose angel announced to you God's plan for salvation
* whose plan for salvation began with your *fiat*—"Let it be done to me as you have said" (Luke 1:38b)
* whose conception was through the power of the Holy Spirit
* who was the long-awaited Savior
* whose name means "God saves"
* whose reign was promised to be without end

Second Joyful Mystery: Visitation

Transformational Moments

Compassionate response to another's need regardless of inconvenience; receiving unsolicited validation or affirmation from another; being the source of confirmation for another; practicing the art of soul companioning; witnessing steadfast hope through long-suffering; serving as a sponsor or godparent

Rejoice Mary, full of grace, the Lord is with you. Blessed are you among women and blessed is the fruit of your womb, Jesus,

* whose angel confided Elizabeth's pregnancy to you
* who took root in your womb as you traveled into the hill country to visit Elizabeth
* whose presence in your womb caused the baby in Elizabeth's womb to leap with joy

* because of whom Elizabeth greeted you as "most blessed among women and blessed is the fruit of your womb!" (Luke 1:42)
* whose conception was confirmed by Elizabeth
* whom Elizabeth identified as "savior," confirming the name given by the angel at conception
* who was the fulfillment of ancient promises
* because of whom you could declare, "My soul proclaims the greatness of the Lord" (Luke 1:46)
* who grew within you as you tended for three months to the needs of Elizabeth
* whose cousin John was "prophet of the Most High" who went "before the Lord to prepare the way for him" (Luke 1:76)

Third Joyful Mystery: Birth of Jesus

Transformational Moments

Cooperating with lawful authority; accepting inconvenience; experiencing deprivation to provide for loved ones; appreciating gifts equally whether meager or abundant (straw or gold); listening to the advice of others; sharing Jesus with visitors; being hospitable and at home with shepherds or kings; recognizing the Herods in your life; identifying your own Egypt and fleeing to it when your soul feels threatened with destruction

Rejoice Mary, full of grace, the Lord is with you. Blessed are you among women and blessed is the fruit of your womb, Jesus,

* whose conception through the Holy Spirit was confided to Joseph in a dream
* whom ancient prophets foretold would be Emmanuel, God with us
* whose time for delivery coincided with the census decreed by Caesar Augustus

* who was born in a Bethlehem stable since there was no room in the inn
* who was wrapped in swaddling clothes and laid in a manger
* whose birth was heralded by angels who proclaimed, "Today a Savior has been born to you in David's town" (Luke 2:11a)
* whose heavenly host sang: "Glory to God in the highest; peace on earth, for God is blessing humankind" (Luke 2:14)
* who was adored by shepherds and kings
* whose nativity events moved you to treasure all these things and reflect on them
* for whose safety you were advised by the Magi to flee to Egypt

Fourth Joyful Mystery: Presentation

Transformational Moments

Honoring your faith tradition; participating in rituals of faith; fulfilling the requirements of law and expectations of custom; recognizing the Simeons in your life; accepting with open hands

*and heart the two-edged sword of prophecy;
being a prophet for another; receiving the comfort of an Anna in your life; being an Anna for
others; being at the right time and the right place
with life-giving support*

Rejoice Mary, full of grace, the Lord is with you.
Blessed are you among women and blessed is
the fruit of your womb, Jesus,

* ✳ who was circumcised on the eighth day and
  named "Jesus"—the name the angel had
  given him before he was conceived
* ✳ whose parents fulfilled the purification
  laws thirty-three days after his circum-
  cision
* ✳ who was taken to Jerusalem to be pre-
  sented to God, as was the custom
* ✳ for whose consecration you offered a pair
  of turtledoves—the offering of the poor
* ✳ who was proclaimed by Simeon to be
  "the light you will reveal to the nations
  and the glory of your people Israel"
  (Luke 2:32)

* whose coming in time was the long-awaited dream of Simeon
* who was "for the rise or fall of the multitudes of Israel. He shall stand as a sign of contradiction'" (Luke 2:34)
* because of whom your own soul would be pierced, that "the secret thoughts of many may be brought to light" (Luke 2:35b)
* whom Anna, the prophetess, recognized as the promised deliverer
* who returned to Nazareth in Galilee after fulfilling the prescriptions of the law

Fifth Joyful Mystery: Finding Jesus in the Temple

Transformational Moments

Realizing that you have lost someone or something precious; feelings of guilt, self-reproach, and irresponsibility; searching and hoping for recovery; retracing your steps; reliving the past; looking for clues; needing direction; feeling relief at reunion; releasing emotion; respectfully asserting; identifying needs and boundaries; learning from an experience of loss; returning to the temple of your soul to find lost treasure

Rejoice Mary, full of grace, the Lord is with you. Blessed are you among women and blessed is the fruit of your womb, Jesus,

* for whose sake the Innocents were martyred
* who remained with you and Joseph in Egypt until the death of Herod
* who resumed a hidden life in Nazareth after his return from Egypt
* who yearly went up to Jerusalem for the Passover celebration as was your family custom
* who remained behind at the end of the feast when he was twelve years old
* whose absence was undetected for a day's journey
* who was found on the third day in the midst of the teachers, listening to them and asking them questions

* to whom you said, "Son, why have you done this to us? Your father and I were very worried while searching for you" (Luke 2:48)
* who questioned, "Why were you looking for me? Do you not know that I must be in my Father's house?" (Luke 2:49)
* who returned to Nazareth and was obedient to you and "increased in wisdom and age and grace and in favor with God" and human beings (Luke 2:52)

The Mysteries of Light

First Mystery of Light: Baptism in the Jordan

Transformational Moments

Working within existing structures; challenging the status quo; respecting customs, tradition, and ritual; experiencing validation moments—being on the right track, in the right place, at the right time, with the right disposition; knowing myself to be, through the merits of Christ, God's beloved child; grounding decisions in Scripture; experiencing utter rootedness and dependence on Divine Providence; being a prophet for reform; humbly knowing who I am and whose I am; detachment from fame, public opinion, and outcomes; dedication or consecration to God's purposes; being led into spiritual desert experiences; living through desert times in the soul without anesthetizing the pain or filling the void with distraction or creature comforts

Rejoice Mary, full of grace, the Lord is with you. Blessed are you among women and blessed is the fruit of your womb, Jesus,

* about whom the Baptist said, "I baptize you in water as a sign of your conversion, but the one who is coming after me is more powerful than me; indeed I am not worthy to carry his sandals. He will baptize you in the Holy Spirit and fire" (Matthew 3:11)
* who came from Galilee to John at the Jordan to be baptized by him

* whose request for baptism was questioned by John who said, "How is it you come to me: I should be baptized by you!" (Matthew 3:14)
* who advised the Baptist, "Let it be like that for now. We must do justice to God's plan." (Matthew 3:15)
* who emerged from the baptismal waters and "saw the Spirit of God come down like a dove and rest upon him" (Matthew 3:16b)
* at whose baptism a voice from heaven was heard saying, "This is my Son, the Beloved; he is my Chosen One" (Matthew 3:17)
* whom the Spirit led "into the desert to be tempted by the devil" (Matthew 4:1)
* who fasted forty days and forty nights after his baptism in the Jordan
* who withstood the temptations of the devil and said, "People cannot live on bread alone, but on every word that comes from the mouth of God" (Matthew 4:4)

25

✱ who was ministered to by angels after the devil left him

Second Mystery of Light:
Self-Manifestation at the Wedding of Cana

Transformational Moments

Responding to curve balls or inopportune requests; transitioning from reaction to response; anticipating the needs of others; living with a confidence born from intimate knowledge of Jesus; knowing the substance beneath the surface; being called into action by others; responding with compassion and a hundredfold generosity versus mere compliance; detaching from my desired results to let God's take over; standing ready to do as directed without advance knowledge of outcome; being a good steward by naming the facts, identifying the bottom line, providing fullness versus half-way measures

Rejoice Mary, full of grace, the Lord is with you. Blessed are you among women and blessed is the fruit of your womb, Jesus,

✳ who was invited to a wedding in Cana of Galilee, along with his Mother and his disciples

✳ to whom you said, "They have no wine" (John 2:3b)

✳ who said to you, "Woman, your thoughts are not mine! My hour has not yet come" (v. 4)

✳ whom you knew so well that you "said to the servants, 'Do whatever he tells you'" (v. 5)

✳ who directed the servants to fill with water six water jars, each holding fifteen to twenty-five gallons of water

✳ who told the servants to take a sample of the water to the waiter in charge

✳ whose miraculous intervention was validated when the waiter in charge tasted the water-made-wine and said to the bridegroom, "Everyone serves the best wine first and when people have drunk enough, he serves that which is ordinary. Instead you have kept the best wine until the end" (v. 10)

* who worked his first sign at your request
* who manifested his glory when he transformed water into wine
* whose miracle increased the faith of his disciples, and they followed him from the wedding feast to Capernaum

Third Mystery of Light: Proclamation of the Kingdom of God

Transformational Moments

Being willing to put my light where all can see; committing to ongoing conversion; practicing forgiveness, mercy, trust, reconciliation, repentance, and non-judgementalism; living in such a way that Christ may reign through my being, choices, words, and actions

Rejoice Mary, full of grace, the Lord is with you. Blessed are you among women and blessed is the fruit of your womb, Jesus,

* whose birth fulfilled the scripture prophecy that the messiah would be born in

Bethlehem and become a ruler who would shepherd Israel

✻ who "went into Galilee and began preaching the Good News of God. He said, 'The time has come; the kingdom of God is at hand. Change your ways and believe the Good News'" (Mark 1:14-15)

✻ who permitted a sinful woman to wash his feet with her tears and anoint them with fragrant oil

✻ who instructed Simon the Pharisee about love, forgiveness, and compassion when he said, "This is why, I tell you, her sins, her many sins, are forgiven, because of her great love. But the one who is forgiven little, has little love" (Luke 7:47)

✻ who gave new life to the sinful woman with the words, "Your sins are forgiven....Your faith has saved you; go in peace" (vv. 48-50)

✻ whose actions caused the pharisees to comment among themselves: "Now this man claims to forgive sins!" (v. 49)

* who extended his mission of mercy through the apostles when he said, "Receive the Holy Spirit; for those whose sins you forgive, they are forgiven; for those whose sins you retain, they are retained" (John 20:22-23)

* who challenged the self-righteous who intended to stone the adulterous woman when he said, "Let the man among you who has no sin be the first to throw a stone at her" (John 8:7)

* who healed the paralytic with the words, "My son, your sins are forgiven....Stand up, take up your mat and go home" (Mark 2:5-11)

* who said, "Go and find out what this means: *'What I want is mercy, not sacrifice.'* I did not come to call the righteous but sinners" (Matthew 9:13)

Fourth Mystery of Light:
Transfiguration

Transformational Moments

Experiencing mountain-top moments; getting glimpses of the big picture; celebrating glory preceded by suffering; using the inspirations and visions of the present as fuel and nourishment for the journey, without grasping at them; seeing and moving outside the lines; living the now while honoring yesterday and welcoming tomorrow

Rejoice Mary, full of grace, the Lord is with you. Blessed are you among women and blessed is the fruit of your womb, Jesus,

* who, several days after the first prediction of his passion and death, "took Peter, John and James and went up the mountain to pray" (Luke 9:28)
* whose disciples observed that "while he was praying, the aspect of his face was

changed and his clothing become dazzling white" (v. 29)

* who was observed talking with Moses and Elijah about "his departure that had to take place in Jerusalem" (v. 31)

* who was the fulfillment of the Law and the Prophets as symbolized by Moses and Elijah

* to whom Peter said, "Master, how good it is for us to be here for we can make three tents, one for you, one for Moses and one for Elijah" (v. 33)

* whose apostles were overcome with awe by his Transfiguration and were overshadowed by a cloud

* who was validated in the presence of the apostles as they heard a voice from the cloud say, "This is my Son, the Beloved; listen to him" (Mark 9:7)

* who strictly directed the apostles to tell no one what they had experienced until he had first risen from the dead

* whose Transfiguration prepared the disciples to understand that, in the divine plan,

Jesus had to suffer and die before his glory would be manifested in the Holy Spirit
✳ who calls each soul to be transfigured and transformed through participation in his passion, death, and resurrection

Fifth Mystery of Light: Institution of the Eucharist

Transformational Moments

Building upon and incorporating tradition; anticipating a departure or death; preparing loved ones for death or change; articulating values; seeing ordinary elements become divine sustanence; vulnerability; living the truth that we become what we receive; making of self bread for others; placing on the paten and in the chalice the hopes, fears, needs, and emptiness to be transformed; feeding on relationship; becoming communion to heal isolation

Rejoice Mary, full of grace, the Lord is with you. Blessed are you among women and blessed is the fruit of your womb, Jesus,

* who celebrated the Passover meal with his disciples
* who "realized that his hour had come to pass from this world to the Father" (John 13:1b)
* who "loved those who were his own in the world" and who "would love them with perfect love" (v. 1c-d)
* who rose from the table and washed the feet of his disciples
* who commissioned the apostles for service by saying, "If I, then, your *Lord* and Master, have washed your feet, you also must wash one another's feet. I have just given you an example that as I have done, you also may do" (vv. 14-15)
* who assured us that "whoever welcomes the one I send, welcomes me, and whoever welcomes me, welcomes the One who sent me" (v. 20)
* who at his Last Supper spoke of our relationship with the Father, the coming of the Holy Spirit, and his own return in glory (John 14)

* who "took bread, said a blessing and broke it, and gave it to his disciples saying, 'Take and eat; this is my body'" (Matthew 26:26)

* who "took a cup and gave thanks, and passed it to them saying, 'Drink this, all of you, for this is my blood, the blood of the Covenant, which is poured out for many for the forgiveness of sins" (vv. 27-28)

* who said, "I am the living *bread which has come from heaven*; whoever eats of this bread will live forever. The bread I shall give is my flesh and I shall give it for the life of the world" (John 6:51)

The Sorrowful Mysteries

First Sorrowful Mystery:
Agony in the Garden

Transformational Moments

Desiring support but having to go it alone; requesting help but meeting disappointment instead; experiencing human inadequacy, betrayal, the abuse of intimacy, and abandonment; struggling to make a decision; resigning oneself to the will of God; deserting another in time of need; letting down a loved one; giving into personal comfort when sacrifice is required; reacting out of fear rather than responding out of love

Rejoice Mary, full of grace, the Lord is with you. Blessed are you among women and blessed is the fruit of your womb, Jesus,

* who desired to eat the Passover Supper with his apostles
* who gave an example of service by washing the feet of his apostles
* who predicted his betrayal and excused Judas from the supper
* who consecrated bread and wine into his body and blood
* whose last discourse focused on the importance of love manifested in action
* who went with his apostles to the Garden

of Gethsemane after the supper, as was their custom

* who confided that his soul was sorrowful and asked his friends to pray with him
* who experienced an agony of blood as he prayed that the cup might pass him by but who resigned himself to the will of the Father
* who returned three times to his friends for comfort and excused their sleeping by saying, "but human nature is weak" (Matthew 26:41b)
* who was betrayed by Judas's kiss

Second Sorrowful Mystery: Scourging at the Pillar

Transformational Moments

Being railroaded or railroading another; experiencing manipulation, deception, double standards, hypocrisy, false accusation, shady operations, or bullying; inflicting harm; experiencing or causing public humiliation; reducing a person to an object

Rejoice Mary, full of grace, the Lord is with you. Blessed are you among women and blessed is the fruit of your womb, Jesus,

* who was taken like a thief in the night for fear of popular reaction
* who was accused of blasphemy at an illegal trial of the Sanhedrin
* who was taken to Pilate since the Jews had no power to put a man to death
* who was interrogated by Pilate and Herod, because neither could find a case against him
* who remained silent before his accusers
* who was stripped and scourged at the pillar
* whose body was pain-racked as bits of flesh were torn apart by the scourging
* who was mocked, tormented, and spit upon
* who was treated with contempt
* whose accusers remained outside the praetorium to avoid ritual impurity

Third Sorrowful Mystery:
Crowning with Thorns

Transformational Moments

Taunting another; being or causing another to be an object of ridicule; making fun of another; deriving pleasure and satisfaction from the hurt borne by another; experiencing emotional and physical abuse; feeling rejection from the very people you help

Rejoice Mary, full of grace, the Lord is with you. Blessed are you among women and blessed is the fruit of your womb, Jesus,

- ✳ who was scourged by the soldiers
- ✳ who was wrapped in a scarlet military cloak and made to play the fool
- ✳ whose head was pierced with a crown of thorns and in whose right hand was placed a reed for a scepter
- ✳ who was mocked, spit at, struck with the reed, and taunted as "King of the Jews"

* who was stripped of the cloak, dressed in his own clothes, and led back to Pilate
* whose condition moved Pilate to say, "Here is the man!" (John 19:5)
* who was less valued than the robber Barabbas
* who "like a lamb led to the slaughter or a sheep before the shearer he did not open his mouth" (Isaiah 53:7b)
* at whose sight the mob shouted, "Crucify him!" (John 19:6)

Fourth Sorrowful Mystery: Carrying the Cross

Transformational Moments

Engaging in non-resistance; experiencing unjust punishment; cooperating with consequences; offering compassion in the midst of one's own suffering; accepting help; refusing to retaliate; maintaining self-possession, perseverance, and long-suffering; kicking another when they are down; being like Simon of Cyrene for another; practicing the sensitivity and courage of Veronica

Rejoice Mary, full of grace, the Lord is with you.
Blessed are you among women and blessed is
the fruit of your womb, Jesus,

* who was sentenced to death at the hour
  at which the priests began to slaughter
  Passover lambs in the temple
* who accepted the cross in silence and
  began his Via Dolorosa through the narrow
  streets to Golgatha
* whose weakened human condition made
  the cross unmanageable
* whose suffering pierced your own soul
* who was given the help of Simon through
  the impure motivation of his tormentors
* who fell, even with the support given by
  Simon
* who was refreshed and affirmed by the
  sensitivity of Veronica
* who showed compassion in his passion
  for the weeping women of Jerusalem
* who was "like a lamb led to the slaughter"
  in fulfillment of the Scripture (Isaiah
  53:7b)

✳ whose will remained resolute despite the
condition of his body

Fifth Sorrowful Mystery:
Crucifixion and Death

Transformational Moments

*Experiencing the irreverent treatment of a per
son; the death of a loved one; the inability t
right a wrong; bereavement; the death of a drean
the loss of innocence; separation, divorce, irre
versible break in a relationship; poor healtl
chronic illness, hospice care, mental illness*

Rejoice Mary, full of grace, the Lord is with you
Blessed are you among women and blessed i
the fruit of your womb, Jesus,

✳ who was stripped of his garments, which
reopened the wounds of his scourging
✳ who prepared to leave the world as he
entered it, with nothing to call his own
✳ who was nailed to the cross without anesthetizing his pain

* who was mounted between two thieves whose punishment was merited
* who promised salvation to the repentant thief
* whose cross became a pulpit, possibly the most powerful of his entire ministry
* for whose garments the soldiers rolled dice
* who hung on the cross in agony from noon until midday
* who was master of his life even at the moment of death, bowing his head before giving up his spirit
* whose inscription read: *"Jesus the Nazorean, King of the Jews"* (John 19:19)

The Glorious Mysteries

First Glorious Mystery: Resurrection

Transformational Moments

Putting the welfare of a person before popular ity or the esteem of others; relieving the stress of another; practicing works of mercy; finding unexpected life after crushing sorrow; receiv ing second chances, forgiveness, or empower ment

Rejoice Mary, full of grace, the Lord is with you. Blessed are you among women and blessed is the fruit of your womb, Jesus,

- ✳ whose bruised, lifeless body you cradled in your arms
- ✳ whose body was prepared for burial by Joseph of Arimathea and Nicodemus, who brought a mixture of myrrh and al oes

* whose body was wrapped in fine linen with perfumed oils and laid in the tomb of Joseph of Arimathea since it was the Jewish Preparation Day
* whose tomb was sealed and guarded by the temple guards
* who rose from the dead on the third day in fulfillment of the Scripture
* whose Resurrection was announced to the women by an angel of the Lord
* who appeared to Mary Magdalene in his resurrected form and spoke her name
* who was seen by his disciples on many occasions after his Resurrection
* who empowered his apostles to forgive sins
* whose Resurrection was doubted by Thomas until he personally saw and touched Jesus

Second Glorious Mystery: Ascension

Transformational Moments

Having grief turned into amazement; receiving new understanding or an "aha!" experience; practicing zeal without counting the cost; catching on to the big picture

Rejoice Mary, full of grace, the Lord is with you. Blessed are you among women and blessed is the fruit of your womb, Jesus,

* who remained with his apostles for forty days after his Resurrection, instructing them and providing opportunities for them to forgive themselves and strengthen their faith
* who opened the minds of the apostles to the understanding of Scripture
* who led the apostles to a mountain near Bethany
* who commissioned his apostles to be

witnesses of his Resurrection to the ends of the earth

✳ who commanded that disciples be made of all nations through baptism

✳ who promised to be with us until the end of the world

✳ who promised to send his Spirit to sustain us

✳ who instructed the apostles to wait in Jerusalem for the coming of the Spirit

✳ who was lifted up before their eyes and vanished from their sight

✳ whose angels asked, "Men of Galilee, why do you stand here looking up at the sky? This Jesus who has been taken from you into heaven will return in the same way as you have seen him go there" (Acts 1:11)

Third Glorious Mystery:
Descent of the Holy Spirit

Transformational Moments

Experiencing fear transformed into courage; witnessing boldly rather than protecting self; allowing growth and personal change; practicing generosity of spirit; depending on God in the midst of chaos; having energy; celebrating and nurturing inner freedom

Rejoice Mary, full of grace, the Lord is with you. Blessed are you among women and blessed is the fruit of your womb, Jesus,

* who called the Spirit the promise of his heavenly Father
* whose apostles "were all together in one place" (Acts 2:1b)
* whose Spirit descended upon the apostles on the day of Pentecost—fifty days after the Resurrection

✳ whose Spirit descended with a strong driving wind that was heard all through the house where they were seated

✳ whose Spirit settled on each of them in the form of a tongue of fire

✳ whose Spirit filled the apostles and made them bold to proclaim as the Spirit prompted them

✳ whose Spirit attracted large crowds of Jews from every nation who were staying in Jerusalem at the time

✳ whose Spirit bestowed gifts of wisdom, understanding, counsel, fortitude, knowledge, piety, and fear of the Lord

✳ whose Spirit empowered the apostles to reveal many signs and wonders among the people

✳ whose Spirit guided the growth of the Early Church

Fourth Glorious Mystery: Assumption

Transformational Moments

Practicing humility, openness, readiness, and responsiveness; anticipating the needs of others; keeping confidences; offering forgiveness; serving as unifier, Christ-bearer, stabilizer, mentor, model, mother, co-redeemer

Rejoice Mary, full of grace, the Lord is with you. Blessed are you among women and blessed is the fruit of your womb, Jesus

* because of whom you were conceived free from original sin
* whose presence in time was possible through your *fiat*
* who took root in your womb and became human
* who was subject to you and taught by you
* who was the cause of your joy

＊ who performed his first miracle at your request in Cana of Galilee

＊ who gave you into the care of John and gave you to us as Mother

＊ who positioned you as Mother of the Church

＊ who preserved your body from corruption

＊ who assumed you, body and soul, into heaven

Fifth Glorious Mystery:
Coronation of Mary

Transformational Moments

Celebrating Mary's titles—Beacon of Hope, Mediatrix of All Grace, Model for the Millennium, Faithful Handmaid of the Lord; living in the spirit of her words: "Let it be done to me", "Do whatever he tells you;" allowing ourselves to be led "to Jesus through Mary"

Rejoice Mary, full of grace, the Lord is with you. Blessed are you among women and blessed is the fruit of your womb, Jesus

* who crowned you Queen of Heaven and Earth
* who put all things under your feet
* who names you Queen of Angels
* who names you Queen of Martyrs, Patriarchs, and Confessors
* who names you Queen of Prophets, Virgins, Apostles, and All Saints

* who crowned you Queen conceived without original sin
* who crowned you Queen assumed into Heaven
* who crowned you Queen of the Most Holy Rosary
* who crowned you Queen of Peace
* because of whom I say with confidence: "My Queen, my mother, remember I am yours."

The Jesus Statements Rosary

To know Jesus is to love Jesus. The gospels help us to know the thoughts of his heart, the sentiments of his soul, his guiding principles, his actions, and his advice. The gospels are the blueprint answer to the question, "What would Jesus do?" You can sit with the gospels and create your own rosary of Jesus statements.

Here are fifty quotations of Jesus that appear in sequence in the Gospel of Matthew, chapters 1 to 12. Now that you are familiar with this way of praying the rosary, the "Rejoice Mary" text will not be repeated before each decade.

Rejoice Mary, full of grace, the Lord is with you. Blessed are you among women and blessed is the fruit of your womb, Jesus, who said

First Decade

* ✳ "Come, follow me, and I will make you fishers of people" (Matthew 4:19)
* ✳ "Fortunate are those who hunger and thirst for justice, for they shall be satisfied" (5:6)
* ✳ "Fortunate are those with a pure heart, for they shall see God" (5:8)
* ✳ "You are the salt of the earth" and "You are the light of the world" (vv. 13a,14a)
* ✳ "In the same way your light must shine before others, so that they may see the good you do and praise your Father in Heaven" (v. 16)
* ✳ "Do not think that I have come to remove the Law and the Prophets. I have not come to remove but to fulfill them" (v. 17)

✳ "I tell you, then, that if you are not righteous in a better way than the teachers of the Law and the Pharisees, you will never enter the kingdom of Heaven" (v. 20)

✳ "Whoever gets angry with his brother will have to face trial" (v. 22a)

✳ "If you are about to offer your gift at the altar and you remember that your brother has something against you, leave your gift there in front of the altar, go at once and make peace with your brother, and then come back and offer your gift to God" (vv. 23-24)

✳ "Say *yes* when you mean *yes* and say *no* when you mean *no*. Anything else you say comes from the devil" (v. 37)

Second Decade

✳ "Do not oppose evil with evil" (5:39a)

✳ "Love your enemies, and pray for those who persecute you (v. 44)

✳ "If you love those who love you, what is special about that? Do not even tax collectors do as much?" (v. 46)

* "For your part you shall be righteous and perfect in the way your heavenly Father is righteous and perfect" (v. 48)
* "Be careful not to make a show of your righteousness before people" (6:1a)
* "If you give something to the poor, do not let your left hand know what your right hand is doing, so that your gift remains really secret. Your Father who sees what is kept secret, will reward you" (vv. 3-4)
* "When you pray, go into your room, close the door and pray to your Father who is with you in secret; and your Father who see what is kept secret will reward you" (v. 6)
* "Your Father knows what you need, even before you ask him" (v. 8b)
* "Our Father in Heaven,..." (vv. 9-13)
* "For you can know a tree by its fruit" (12:33b)

Third Decade

* "If you forgive others their wrongs, your Father in Heaven will also forgive yours. If you do not forgive others, then your Father will not forgive you either" (6:14-15)

* "When you fast, wash your face and make yourself look cheerful" (v. 17)

* "Do not store up treasure for yourself here on earth where moth and rust destroy it" (v. 19a)

* "For where your treasure is, there also your heart will be" (v. 21)

* "No one can serve two masters" (v. 24a)

* "Set your heart first on the kingdom and justice of God and all these things will also be given to you" (v. 33)

* "Do not worry about tomorrow for tomorrow will worry about itself. Each day has enough trouble of its own" (v. 34)

* "Do not judge and you will not be judged" (7:1)

* "Why do you look at the speck in your

brother's eye and not see the plank in your own eye?" (v. 3)

✳ "Ask and you will receive; seek and you will find; knock and the door will be opened" (v. 7)

Fourth Decade

✳ "Go home now. As you believed, so let it be" (Matthew 8:13a)

✳ "Foxes have holes and birds have nests, but the Son of Man has nowhere to lay his head" (v. 20)

✳ "Why are you so afraid, you of little faith?" (v. 26a)

✳ "Go and find out what this means, '*What I want is mercy, not sacrifice*'" (9:13a)

✳ "I did not come to call the righteous but sinners" (v. 13b)

✳ "You don't put new wine in old wine-skins. If you do, the wineskins will burst and the wine be spilt. No, you put new wine in fresh skins; then both are preserved" (v. 17)

✳ "The harvest is abundant but the workers

are only few. Ask the master of the harvest to send workers to gather his harvest" (vv. 37-38)

✳ "You received this as a gift, so give it as a gift" (10:8b)

✳ "A worker deserves his living" (v. 10:10b)

✳ "You must be cleaver as snakes and innocent as doves" (v. 16b)

Fifth Decade

✳ "But when you are arrested, do not worry about what you are to say and how you are to say it; when the hour comes, you will be given what you are to say" (Matthew 10:19)

✳ "Do not be afraid of those who kill the body, but not the person. Rather be afraid of him who can destroy both body and soul in hell" (v. 28)

✳ "He who cares only for his own life will lose it; he who loses his life for my sake will find it" (v. 39)

✳ "And I promise you if anyone gives even

a cup of cold water to one of these little ones because he is a disciple of mine, he will not go unrewarded" (v. 42)

✳ "And how fortunate is the one who does not take offense at me" (Matthew 11:6)

✳ "I tell you this: no one greater than John the Baptist has appeared among the sons of women, and yet the least in the kingdom of Heaven is greater than he" (v. 11)

✳ "Yet they will see that—Wisdom did everything well" (v. 19b)

✳ "Come to me, all you who work hard and who carry heavy burdens and I will refresh you" (v. 28)

✳ "Take my yoke upon you and learn from me for I am gentle and humble of heart; and you will find rest" (v. 29)

✳ "Whoever does the will of my Father in Heaven is for me brother, sister, or mother" (Matthew 12:50)

How to Create Rosary Meditations from Your Reading of Scripture

Create rosary styles of your own. As you read Scripture and find verses you like and want to pray over, slot them into the appropriate categories, for example,

> of whom it was said…
> because of whom…
> to whom it was said…
> who was asked…
> who initiated…
> with whom…
> for whom…
> from whom…

The following meditations illustrate some variations. With Scripture in hand, possibilities multiply.

Of Whom It Was Said...
(from the Gospel of Matthew)

Rejoice, Mary, full of grace, the Lord is with you. Blessed are you among women and blessed is the fruit of your womb, Jesus, of whom it was said

* "You are to call [him] 'Jesus' for he will save his people from their sins" (1:21)
* "Where is the newborn king of the Jews?" (2:2a)
* "This is my Son, the Beloved; he is my Chosen One" (3:17)
* "What kind of man is he? Even the winds and the sea obey him" (8:27)
* "Why is it that your master eats with those sinners and tax collectors?" (9:11)
* "This is my Son, the Beloved, my Chosen One. Listen to him" (17:5)
* "The people who walked ahead of Jesus and those who followed him began to shout: *"Hosanna to the Son of David! Blessed is he who comes in the name of*

the Lord! Hosanna, glory in the high-est!" (21:9)

✳ "This is the Prophet Jesus from Nazareth of Galilee" (21:11)

✳ "Truly, this man was a Son of God!" (27:54b)

✳ "He is not here, for he is raised as he said" (28:6a)

✳ "He is risen from the dead and is going ahead of you to Galilee" (28:7)

Who...(from the Gospel of Mark)

✳ sought baptism by John in the Jordan (1:9)

✳ fasted and prayed in the desert (v. 12)

✳ went to Galilee and preached the Good News (v. 14)

✳ called Simon and Andrew to fish for human beings (v. 17)

✳ taught with authority in the synagogue of Capernaum (vv. 21-22)

✳ cured a man with an unclean spirit (v. 25)

* healed Peter's mother-in-law (v. 31)
* healed many that were sick and forbade the devils to speak of him (v. 34)
* rose early in the morning to go to a solitary place to pray (v. 35)
* preached in the synagogues throughout Galilee and cast out devils (v. 39)